Christian Q&A Book for Kids

CHRISTIAN Q&A BOOK FOR KIDS

100+ Questions and Answers about God and the Bible

Amy Houts

ROCKRIDGE
PRESS

For my grandchildren, Charlotte, Jacob, and Toby.
May you find answers here.

First Rockridge Press trade paperback edition 2022

For general information on our other products and services, please contact our Customer Care Department within the United States at (866) 744-2665, or outside the United States at (510) 253-0500.

Paperback ISBN: 978-1-68539-091-4
eBook ISBN: 978-1-68539-481-3

Manufactured in the United States of America

Interior and Cover Designer: Jane Archer and Alex Klawitter
Art Producer: Hannah Dickerson
Editor: Sasha Henriques
Production Editor: Cassie Gitkin
Production Manager: Lanore Coloprisco

All images used under license from Shutterstock.com and iStock.com, except for the following: © Amir Abou Roumié, p. VI (pen); © Joel & Ashley Selby, p. VII (pencil)

Author photo courtesy of Bob Delsol

10 9 8 7 6 5 4 3 2 1 0

Contents

A LETTER TO ADULTS

Hi! I'm Amy, an award-winning Christian author of over one hundred children's books. I'm also a grandparent. I chose topics for this book related to Christian values and beliefs, and I included the biblical basis for the answers. This book is intended to be a jumping-off point for a larger discussion. The section for kids to write their own questions in the back of this book will encourage them to seek answers together with you. The discussion guide, also in the back of the book, will lead you through that process. Through your conversations, children will gain a deeper understanding of God, the Bible, and themselves. I hope you both find this book to be a valuable resource.

A LETTER TO KIDS

Hi! My name is Amy. I want you to know it's okay to have questions about God! I wrote this book to help you find answers about God, the Bible, and religion. If you have a question that you don't see answered, there's a section in the back for you to write it down so you can find the answer on your own. Let's get started!

100+
Questions and Answers

Who is God?

God is love! Like your parents and caregivers, God looks after you. He loves you and wants the best for you. In fact, we often call God "Father," but He is different from your father and mother on Earth. God is your heavenly Father. God is everywhere, omnipresent. God is all-knowing, omniscient. God is all-powerful, omnipotent. He is the One we pray to and worship. God is kind, good, merciful, and more. He cares for you so much! A letter written by Jesus's friend John tells us who God is. 1 John 4:8 says, "Whoever does not love does not know God, because God is love."

Who created God?

No one made or created God. This is hard to understand because we think about Him in our limited, human way. He exists, or lives, outside of time. He exists outside of space. Colossians 1:17 says, "He is before all things, and in him all things hold together." Notice how the Bible verse says God "is." That's because God is, was, and always will be here.

Why did God create Earth?

Creativity comes in many forms. We can create art, music, food, and so much more. God is creative, too. Some people call God "the Creator," as in, "the One who creates." He created the heavens and the earth and everything we would need to live here, to share His life. Romans 11:36 says, "For from him and through him and for him are all things." How? Psalm 33:9 says that God created everything using His words and His commands: "For he spoke, and it came to be; he commanded, and it stood firm."

 ## Will God be here forever?

 Do the adults in your life ever talk about what it was like when they were a child, before the internet and cell phones? Even though that was a long time ago, God was there. And long, long before that, before cars and light bulbs, God was there. Think about the future when you grow up. Will we go to school on hoverboards or travel to Mars? God will be there, too. The word "everlasting" means "forever," "always," and "endless." Psalm 90:2 says, "Before the mountains were born or you brought forth the whole world, from everlasting to everlasting you are God." God has no beginning and no end. He's eternal. He will be here forever.

Why hasn't anyone seen God?

God is spirit. He doesn't have a body. That's how God can be everywhere. Acts 17:24 says, "God who made the world and everything in it is the Lord of heaven and earth and does not live in temples built by human hands." The Bible tells us God has been seen in a real sense in different forms on Earth—as a burning bush, as an angel, and as a man, Jesus. We can also "see" God in another sense, like in the adorableness of a puppy, in the great taste of chocolate, and in the sound of a friend's laugh.

Is God real?

The word "real" means "actual" or "true." It's hard to believe something is real if you can't see it. Think of how you can't see the wind, but you know it's there. We can't see God, but we know He's real in the way He shows or reveals Himself to us. One reason we know God is real is because we are made in His image, His likeness, as we learn in Genesis 5:1: "When God created mankind, he made them in the likeness of God." If we are real, He is real!

What if I doubt that God is real?

It's okay to doubt that God is real! Doubt is when you are not sure if something is true. That's good! It shows that you are curious and that you are thinking about what you believe. Even Jesus's friends had doubts. Do you know about the miracle when Jesus walked on the water? Peter started walking on water, too, toward Jesus, but then he started thinking, *This can't be possible!* and began sinking. Matthew 14:31 says, "Immediately Jesus reached out his hand and caught him. 'You of little faith,' he said, 'why did you doubt?'" Faith overcomes doubt. Reading the Bible can build your faith.

Does God know what's going to happen in the future?

Think of it this way: You want to have a picnic. You plan the location and what to bring. You don't know what you'll say or who you'll meet, but you know where you're going. God is like that: He knows where we are headed, but He lets us plan our route and handle our own challenges along the way, like rain or ants at a picnic. He's by our side every step of the way. While it's easy to get confused about how God controls our future and how our own decisions shape our path, we can trust that God is always taking care of us. Proverbs 16:9 explains, "In their hearts humans plan their course, but the Lord establishes their steps."

Does God's plan for me ever change?

God's plan, or His will, is something that He knows and that we can try to discern, or figure out. There are times in the Old Testament when it seems like God changes His mind. Exodus 32:14 says, "Then the Lord relented and did not bring on his people the disaster he had threatened." (Lucky for them!) But Psalm 33:11 says, "But the plans of the Lord stand firm forever, the purposes of his heart through all generations." We all have a path. We don't have to worry about whether God's will or plan changes because we know He is guiding us the whole time. Jeremiah 29:11 assures us, "'For I know the plans I have for you,' declares the Lord, 'plans to prosper you and not to harm you, plans to give you hope and a future.'"

Does God know what I'm thinking?

Special friends understand us. They seem to know what we're thinking before we tell them. God is like a special friend. He understands you. Even though God already knows what you're thinking, He wants you to talk to Him. You can be thankful God knows your thoughts because then He can guide you. Psalm 139:1–2 says, "You have searched me, Lord, and you know me. You know when I sit and when I rise; you perceive my thoughts from afar." God knows you better than you know yourself!

Does God really care about me?

There may be times when you think that God doesn't care about you. But that's never the way God feels! You are His child. He loves you more than you can know or understand. You are so precious and important to God! He is with you, watching over you right now. He has been watching over you since you were a baby. And He always will. Take comfort in Psalm 121:8: "The Lord will watch over your coming and going both now and forevermore."

Does God make mistakes?

Have you ever given the wrong answer to a question? Maybe you didn't know the answer. God knows all the answers to all the questions. Maybe you weren't paying attention. God is always paying attention. Maybe you made the wrong decision. God is able to make the right decision about everything. He has all the information He needs for every situation. There are times God feels bad about things, like when people sinned in Genesis 6:6, "and his heart was deeply troubled," but that doesn't mean He made a mistake by creating them. Psalm 18:30 explains, "As for God, his way is perfect: The Lord's word is flawless." So, no, God never makes mistakes. God can't make mistakes!

Sometimes I make mistakes and I can hardly forgive myself. Will God always forgive me?

God's love is unconditional. There is nothing you can do that He won't forgive! Psalm 103:10–11 reminds us, "He does not treat us as our sins deserve or repay us according to our iniquities. For as high as the heavens are above the earth, so great is his love for those who fear him." Here, "iniquities" means "wrongdoings," and "fear him" means "those who follow him." If God can forgive us of anything, we need to forgive ourselves of our mistakes, too!

What is God's forgiveness like?

When God forgives you, it's not like when a person forgives you. Let's say a friend was not nice. They say they're sorry, and you forgive them. But you might not forget what they did. You might not feel the same about your friendship. God's forgiveness is not like that. God forgives you completely! Isaiah 43:25 talks about transgressions, which are sins. God says, "I, even I, am he who blots out your transgressions, for my own sake, and remembers your sins no more." If you are truly sorry, God forgives you and He forgets what you did wrong.

 **Can I ask for forgiveness from God more than once?**

 Matthew 18:21–22 says, "Then Peter came to Jesus and asked, 'Lord, how many times shall I forgive my brother or sister who sins against me? Up to seven times?' Jesus answered, 'I tell you, not seven times, but seventy-seven times.'" Jesus doesn't mean that you need to keep track and count to seventy-seven. He means that you should just keep forgiving! God will keep forgiving you, too. But if you must ask God for forgiveness over and over, figure out why. Are you truly sorry for what you did? If so, it's time to see how and what you can do to change so you don't have to keep asking.

What if God forgets about me?

God could never forget about you because He is a part of you. Sure, it might feel like you've been forgotten when things aren't going well. In Deuteronomy 31:6, God said, "Be strong and courageous. Do not be afraid or terrified because of them, for the Lord your God goes with you; he will never leave you nor forsake you." The word "forsake" is even stronger than "forget." When God says he will never forsake you, He means that He will never turn away from you, abandon you, or leave you unprotected. If you feel like God has forgotten you, pray even harder. Ask Him to help you and show you what you can do to feel closer to Him.

Does God want me to share my things?

God wants you to be kind, and that includes sharing. That doesn't mean sharing everything or always sharing. You might have a special toy you don't want to share. But you can share other things like love and hope. You can be generous and give "a good measure." That means to give more than someone expects. In Luke 6:38, Jesus said, "Give, and it will be given to you. A good measure, pressed down, shaken together and running over, will be poured into your lap. For with the measure you use, it will be measured to you." Share, and people will be more likely to share with you.

Does God want me to be happy?

Yes! God wants you to be happy! What matters is where you look for happiness. Sometimes people think something will make them happy. Then they get it, and they aren't happy. Happiness doesn't come from having more toys, more friends, or more money. True happiness comes from trusting God and His purpose in your life. True happiness comes from seeking God's will for your life. A wise king named Solomon wrote in Ecclesiastes 3:12, "I know that there is nothing better for people than to be happy and to do good while they live."

 ## Does God love me when I'm angry?

 God loves you no matter what you are feeling! He loves you when you are happy, sad, calm, or angry. God loves you *all* the time. Feelings are part of being human; everyone feels angry sometimes. What's important is what you *do* with your anger. Feeling angry might make you want to do something unkind. Ephesians 4:26 says, "'In your anger do not sin': Do not let the sun go down while you are still angry." God wants you to deal with anger in a good way, like using your words to make things right as soon as possible. Fixing what makes you angry can make you happy again!

Why does God let bad things happen to nice people?

God loves us so much that He gives us free will. That means God doesn't control us. He lets people decide what they will say and do. Some of these things are bad. Bad things happen to both nice and not-so-nice people. James 1:2–3 says, "Consider it pure joy, my brothers and sisters, whenever you face trials of many kinds, because you know that the testing of your faith produces perseverance." Here's a surprise: James says we should be happy about our "trials," or the bad stuff that happens. He says they test our faith and keep us going.

 **Does God love people who do bad things?**

 You might think God doesn't love people who are evil. How could He? But He does. Each person is precious to God. He knows it's not the person who is bad but that the person is doing bad things. God knows we are more than our thoughts, feelings, words, or actions. Ephesians 3:17–18 says, "And I pray that you, being rooted and established in love, may have power, together with all the Lord's holy people, to grasp how wide and long and high and deep is the love of Christ." God's love can change people, helping them do and be good.

Who is Jesus?

Christians believe Jesus is God's Son. They believe Jesus was born as a baby just like you and me and lived on Earth over two thousand years ago. He had human parents: a mother named Mary and a father named Joseph. John 1:14 says, "The Word became flesh and made his dwelling among us. We have seen his glory, the glory of the one and only Son, who came from the Father, full of grace and truth." The phrase "the Word became flesh" means God became human. People called "Christians" still follow Jesus's teachings about love and forgiveness.

 **Is "Christ" Jesus's last name?**

 People didn't always have last names. When Jesus lived, people were called by their first name. Many times, a parent's name or the place where they lived was added as a way to identify them. (I'd be Amy of Arthur since that's my dad's name or Amy of Maryville, since that's where I live. What would your name be?) This wasn't true of Jesus. He is also called "Christ" because it means "Messiah." That's someone who makes the world a better place. In Acts 10:36, Peter tells how: "You know the message God sent to the people of Israel, announcing the good news of peace through Jesus Christ, who is Lord of all."

What are some different names for Jesus?

Do you have a nickname, like "Champ" or "Kimmy"? People call Jesus other names, too, based on what He does or who He is to them. Jesus is called "Lord," which is a ruler with great power. Jesus is also called the "Bread of Life," "Redeemer," "Savior," and more. Isaiah 9:6 lists four names for Jesus: "For to us a child is born, to us a son is given, and the government will be on his shoulders. And he will be called Wonderful Counselor, Mighty God, Everlasting Father, Prince of Peace."

Did Jesus's mother know He was God's Son?

Yes, she did! In fact, an angel visited Mary and told her Jesus was God's Son. In Luke 1:31–32, the angel says, "You will conceive and give birth to a son, and you are to call him Jesus. He will be great and will be called the Son of the Most High." Mary was very surprised and must have felt overwhelmed. As the angel explained, Mary tried to understand. She accepted his words as a servant of God. An angel helped Joseph, the man Mary would marry, understand, too. Joseph was also visited by an angel and told about Jesus.

What is the Trinity?

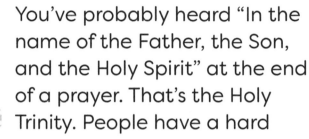

You've probably heard "In the name of the Father, the Son, and the Holy Spirit" at the end of a prayer. That's the Holy Trinity. People have a hard time understanding the Trinity because it's three people in one. God the Father is God. Jesus, or the Son of God, is God. The Holy Spirit is God, too. All three—Father, Son, and Holy Spirit—are part of the same wonderful being. God the Father sent His Son, Jesus, to Earth. The Holy Spirit was sent to live in those who believe in Jesus. In 2 Corinthians 13:14, Paul writes, "May the grace of the Lord Jesus Christ, and the love of God, and the fellowship of the Holy Spirit be with you all."

What is the Holy Spirit?

God promised to send a helper so we could remember what Jesus said and did. The Holy Spirit is that helper! If you ask Him, the Holy Spirit can live in you and guide you. Some people call the Holy Spirit "the Holy Ghost," but that doesn't mean He's like a scary ghost that haunts you; it just means that He's invisible. In John 14:26, Jesus tells his friends, "But the Advocate, the Holy Spirit, whom the Father will send in my name, will teach you all things and will remind you of everything I have said to you."

What is a miracle?

A miracle is something great that happens that can't be explained. It is a sign of God's power. Once there were about five thousand hungry people in a crowd, but there were only five loaves of bread and two fish to feed them. Luke 9:16–17 tells us how Jesus performed a miracle: "Taking the five loaves and the two fish and looking up to heaven, he gave thanks and broke them. Then he gave them to the disciples to distribute to the people. They all ate and were satisfied, and the disciples picked up twelve basketfuls of broken pieces that were left over." It was because of the power of God's love.

What miracles did Jesus do?

There are so many! For example, Jesus told a man who couldn't move for thirty-eight years to get up and walk. And the man walked! Jesus rubbed a blind man's eyes with mud, and the man could see again! Jesus ordered a fever to leave a sick woman, and she became well! He healed many sick people because He cared, He felt compassion, and He knew He could help. Jesus also walked on water, calmed a storm, and brought back to life someone who had died. Miracles helped prove that Jesus was God's Son. Matthew 19:26 says, "Jesus looked at them and said, 'With man this is impossible, but with God all things are possible.'"

Why did the disciples follow Jesus?

Do you have a friend who is kind and smart and fun? You probably enjoy being with that friend. People enjoyed being with Jesus. He was special! People left their homes, their work, and their families to follow Him. When people saw His miracles, they couldn't *not* follow Him! Some heard a new king was coming to save the world and wanted to be a part of it. John 8:12 says, "When Jesus spoke again to the people, he said, 'I am the light of the world. Whoever follows me will never walk in darkness, but will have the light of life.'" Darkness is a symbol for evil. People wanted to follow the light!

What's the difference between a disciple and an apostle?

In Jesus's day, there were twelve special disciples, or followers, whom He called His "apostles": Peter, Andrew, James, James the Younger, John, Philip, Bartholomew, Thomas, Matthew, Thaddaeus, Simon, and Judas. (Paul came later.) These special twelve traveled and taught with Jesus. They are referred to as both "disciples" and "apostles." A disciple follows and learns from Jesus. An apostle goes out and tells or preaches what they've learned. The twelve apostles were disciples first, but not all disciples are apostles. Today, apostles are called "missionaries." Missionaries are sent to help people and tell them about Jesus. Mark 3:14 talks about the twelve apostles: "He appointed twelve that they might be with him and that he might send them out to preach."

Am I a disciple?

If you believe in Jesus and follow His teachings, you are His disciple. In Matthew 4:19–20, Jesus spoke to some fishermen: "'Come, follow me,' Jesus said, 'and I will send you out to fish for people.' At once they left their nets and followed him." Jesus didn't mean that He wanted them to catch people in their fishing nets. He wanted them to learn about a loving God.

What is a parable?

A parable is a story that teaches a lesson. Jesus taught His followers by using parables. Luke 13:18–19 tells a parable: "Then Jesus asked, 'What is the kingdom of God like? What shall I compare it to? It is like a mustard seed, which a man took and planted in his garden. It grew and became a tree, and the birds perched in its branches.'" A tiny seed growing into a huge tree is a symbol for the kingdom of God. It started off small with Jesus and His disciples but grew large with many believers—and it is still growing today!

What is the most important thing Jesus taught?

The most important thing Jesus taught was about love. John 15:12 says, "My command is this: Love each other as I have loved you." Jesus showed people that God was a loving God to adore, not a vengeful God to be feared. Jesus modeled a deep, unselfish love for people by helping them—and we can, too. It's called "serving others." By loving others, Jesus showed His love for us. In showing us how to love others, He taught us about God's amazing kingdom. Jesus loved us *so much,* He gave His life for us.

What does it mean to serve others?

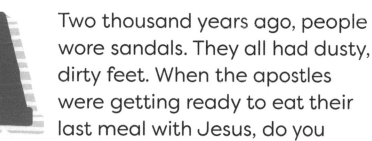

Two thousand years ago, people wore sandals. They all had dusty, dirty feet. When the apostles were getting ready to eat their last meal with Jesus, do you know what Jesus did? He washed their feet! In John 13:14, Jesus says, "Now that I, your Lord and Teacher, have washed your feet, you also should wash one another's feet." Jesus was showing us more than how to act. He was showing us how to think and feel. We need to be humble, not proud, to do the work of a servant, like Jesus did. When you look, you will find lots of ways to help and to serve God.

Does Jesus understand how I feel?

Jesus knows how you feel because, as a human, He felt that way, too. Bible stories show Jesus was sad, angry, tired, and happy. After His friend Lazarus died, Jesus felt sad. He cried. When Jesus saw religious leaders cheating, He felt angry and pushed over the tables in the temple. After being with crowds of people, Jesus felt tired and went alone to pray. A week before He died, Jesus rode into Jerusalem. He felt such strong love for the people there. Luke 19:41 says, "As he approached Jerusalem and saw the city, he wept over it."

Did Jesus ever disobey His parents?

Remember, Jesus is God. He doesn't make mistakes! But He was human. Once, when Jesus was twelve years old, He traveled to Jerusalem with His family. As Jews, they went every year to celebrate the Jewish holiday of Passover. Afterward, Jesus's parents started for home. But they couldn't find Jesus. They looked for three days. They found Him in the local temple. His parents were upset. Although Jesus didn't disobey them, there was a misunderstanding. Jesus responded to His parents in Luke 2:49, calling the temple His "Father's house": "'Why were you searching for me?' he asked. 'Didn't you know I had to be in my Father's house?'"

Why did God let His Son die?

God loves His Son, Jesus. I imagine God was very sad when Jesus died. But it was part of God's plan to save people from sin. God sent Jesus to Earth so we could be forgiven for our sins and our relationship with God could be restored. That's why God was willing to part with His Son. It was for you and me. 1 John 4:9 says, "This is how God showed his love among us: He sent his one and only Son into the world that we might live through him."

How did Jesus come back to life?

Sadly, everyone will pass away one day. We know when people, animals, and other living things die, they don't come back to life. It was different with Jesus. He was human, like you and me, but He was also God. So when Jesus died, He was able to come back to life. Coming back to life is called "resurrection." Jesus lives again! How do we know? 1 Corinthians 15:6 says that lots of people saw Jesus alive after He died: "After that, he appeared to more than five hundred of the brothers and sisters."

What did Jesus do after He was resurrected?

Besides appearing to big crowds of people, Jesus appeared to small groups. The first person was a woman named Mary Magdalene who visited Jesus's tomb. He also appeared to the disciples and ate breakfast with some fishermen. Seeing Jesus alive gave people hope. One of Jesus's main goals was to use the miracle of His resurrection to get more people to turn to God. In Matthew 28:19, Jesus said, "Therefore go and make disciples of all nations, baptizing them in the name of the Father and of the Son and of the Holy Spirit." Jesus wanted everyone to know about salvation. He stayed on Earth for forty days. Then the disciples watched as Jesus rose through the air up to heaven.

Why do people wear cross necklaces?

The cross is a symbol of Jesus, reminding people of how He died. Wearing a cross necklace helps people feel closer to Jesus and to God. It makes them feel loved and safe. Jesus talked about carrying a cross as a symbol of taking on our own burdens, of doing something right even when it's hard. That takes effort, of course, but we always try to do our best. Matthew 16:24 shows Jesus telling His friends how to follow Him: "Then Jesus said to his disciples, 'Whoever wants to be my disciple must deny themselves and take up their cross and follow me.'"

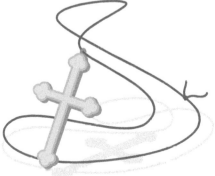

Can anyone believe in Jesus?

Yes! Anyone can believe in Jesus. Romans 10:4 says, "Christ is the culmination of the law so that there may be righteousness for everyone who believes." In order to be righteous, or good, you don't need to *do* anything. You don't need to act a certain way or follow specific rules. The only thing you need to do is believe! Everyone has the choice to believe Jesus is God's Son. Everyone has the choice to believe that Jesus died to save us.

Is it okay to tell my friend about Jesus?

When you're excited about something, you might want your friends to know! Keep in mind, though, people practice many different religions, and they might feel it's a private topic. You might first ask their permission to talk about yours. If they answer no, let it go. If they answer yes, then go ahead and share your beliefs! You might start by saying that God loves everyone. John the Baptist knew Jesus and called Him a "light" because Jesus helped people see the truth. John 1:7 talks about John the Baptist sharing about Jesus with his friends: "He came as a witness to testify concerning that light, so that through him all might believe."

I'm sometimes embarrassed to talk about my faith. Is that wrong?

It's not uncommon to be shy when it comes to talking about your faith. Your personal faith might be something you want to keep to yourself. After all, it's between you and God, not anyone else. It's more important to *live* your faith and let people see Christ in you without ever having to mention His name! Ephesians 4:29 agrees, saying, "Do not let any unwholesome talk come out of your mouths, but only what is helpful for building others up according to their needs, that it may benefit those who listen."

Will my friend who doesn't believe in Jesus go to heaven?

You might have heard that only people who believe in Jesus go to heaven. That might make you worried about your friend. You might tell your friend about your concerns, but know your friend's salvation is up to them. John 12:47 reminds us that Jesus said, "If anyone hears my words but does not keep them, I do not judge that person. For I did not come to judge the world, but to save the world." A loving God will show compassion to your friend.

What is Christianity?

Christianity is a religion. A religion is a system of beliefs. People who follow Christianity are called "Christians." They believe Jesus Christ is the Son of God, and they believe in His teachings. The Bible is their sacred text. The focus of Christianity is to worship God through Jesus. Psalm 95:6 says, "Come, let us bow down in worship, let us kneel before the Lord our Maker." In the past, people didn't always agree on how to worship, so they divided into groups. If you think of Christianity as a tree, it has three main branches: Catholic, Protestant, and Orthodox. Protestants are divided further, and each have their own churches. All of these churches are Christian since their followers believe in Christ.

Is Christianity like other religions?

Christianity is one of many religions in the world. It's similar to other religions in some ways. Many people who follow a religion worship a higher power—Christians worship God. Some religions have special books called "sacred texts." Christians have a sacred text called the Bible, which contains the Old Testament and the New Testament. Religious people often attend worship services in special buildings. Christians hold worship services in special buildings called "churches." It's important to remember what unites us—how we are alike—instead of focusing on what divides us. God loves all of us; after all, just like 1 Corinthians 14:33 says, "For God is not a God of disorder but of peace—as in all the congregations of the Lord's people."

How is Christianity different from other religions?

One main difference between Christianity and other religions relates to worshipping God and Jesus. Some people believe we all worship the same God, but others don't agree. Some religions worship more than one god. Some religions follow the teachings of a wise leader. Another main difference is how members get to heaven, if that religion has a heaven. In some religions, it depends on how people act. In Christianity, it depends on believing that Jesus is the Son of God. Even though we have differences, God wants us to support each other. 1 Thessalonians 5:11 says, "Therefore encourage one another and build each other up, just as in fact you are doing."

What does it mean to be a Christian?

If you believe Jesus Christ is the Son of God, you are a Christian. It's that simple. Notice the word "Christ" makes up the first six letters of the word "Christian"; the word literally means "follower of Christ." A Christian follows Christ and wants to know Him. To know Jesus, you need to read and understand not only what He taught but also what He did. Being a Christian means you have faith in Jesus. You believe you are redeemed, or free from sin, because Jesus died for you. You are redeemed because you know the truth. John 8:32 says, "Then you will know the truth, and the truth will set you free."

Why does it matter what we believe?

It matters because what you believe affects everything! A belief is something that you accept as true. Your beliefs affect what you think and feel, what you say, and how you act. For example, if you believe in kindness, you will be kind. If you believe in fairness, you won't cheat. James 2:18 says, "But someone will say, 'You have faith; I have deeds.' Show me your faith without deeds, and I will show you my faith by my deeds." This verse means "if you look at all the good things I do—not just my words—you will see I believe in God."

What does it mean to be "saved"?

Have you heard about someone being rescued from a burning building? They were saved from the harm of fire. Being saved by Jesus is like that, but the harm you are saved from is sin and death. When you are saved, you are forgiven for your sins. You are right with God. Being saved from death means you will live forever in heaven with God. What do you need to do to be saved? Acts 16:31 tells us: "They replied, 'Believe in the Lord Jesus, and you will be saved—you and your household.'" Believe in Jesus, and you will be saved. That's all there is to it!

What does it mean to be "born again"?

To be born again doesn't mean you're a baby all over again. Being born again means renewing your faith in God. It's a form of baptism, or re-baptism, so people's sins are forgiven and they can start fresh. Water washes them clean, and their spirit is reborn. Jesus talks about this in John 3:5: "'Very truly I tell you, no one can enter the kingdom of God unless they are born of water and the Spirit.'" Some Christian faiths, like Catholicism and Eastern Orthodox, believe you only have to be baptized once, and that one rebirth lasts forever. Others support a second one to reinforce a commitment to your faith.

What is baptism?

Baptism is a ceremony that uses water to clean, or purify, your spirit. In baptism, water is sprinkled or poured on a person's head, or the person is dunked under water. Getting baptized shows you believe in Jesus and want to follow His teachings. People get baptized at different ages, sometimes as babies. Galatians 3:26–27 explains it this way: "So in Christ Jesus you are all children of God through faith, for all of you who were baptized into Christ have clothed yourselves with Christ."

What does it mean to have faith?

Having faith means you believe in something. Your faith is your belief in God, your belief that He can be trusted. The tricky thing about faith is that it means trusting in something you can't see. Jesus says even a little faith has great power! In Matthew 17:20, Jesus tells His friends, "Truly I tell you, if you have faith as small as a mustard seed, you can say to this mountain, 'Move from here to there,' and it will move. Nothing will be impossible for you."

What is the fruit of the Spirit?

Have you seen an apple tree with lots of ripe, shiny apples? Fruit grows on healthy trees. If you work hard at something and it succeeds, people say your work "bears fruit." If we believe in Jesus and invite the Holy Spirit to live in us, we become better people. The fruit of the Spirit isn't real fruit. It's a symbol for success at being a good person. What do you need to be a good person? Galatians 5:22–23 tells us, "But the fruit of the Spirit is love, joy, peace, forbearance, kindness, goodness, faithfulness, gentleness and self-control." The Holy Spirit can help us with all of those.

What is sin?

When you purposely act in a way that God wouldn't want you to act, it's a sin. For example, lying is a sin. A sin separates you from God. The Bible offers rules and stories that help you know how God wants (or doesn't want) you to act. When you sin, you can confess it, or tell it, to God. "If we confess our sins, he is faithful and just and will forgive us," states 1 John 1:9. Forgiveness restores your relationship with God and helps you do better.

Why is it hard to do what is right?

Sometimes we don't know what is right. But sometimes we know the right thing to do, and we don't want to do it. It might be embarrassing, frustrating, or even a little scary. We don't think we have the strength to do the right thing, but God does. 2 Corinthians 12:9 says, "But he said to me, 'My grace is sufficient for you, for my power is made perfect in weakness.' Therefore I will boast all the more gladly about my weaknesses, so that Christ's power may rest on me." Let God help you do what is right.

What is grace?

Grace is love and forgiveness, a precious gift to you from God. This gift is free. You don't have to pay for it or do anything special to earn it. Grace is generous, more than you would hope for or could imagine. Ephesians 2:8-9 talks about this great gift from God: "For it is by grace you have been saved, through faith—and this is not from yourselves, it is the gift of God—not by works, so that no one can boast." It's already yours!

What is it like in heaven?

Heaven is unlike anything our human minds can imagine. It's a wonderful place where our souls or spirits live after we die. We believe you are reunited with those you love who have died before you. We don't know much more about heaven because people don't visit there—they stay. We do know it's a joyous place where you live forever with God. Jesus's friend John wrote about his vision of heaven in the last book of the Bible. It's described in Revelation 21:4: "He will wipe every tear from their eyes. There will be no more death or mourning or crying or pain, for the old order of things has passed away."

Will I see my pet in heaven?

It's understandable for you to love your pet so much you want to be with it in heaven. The Bible doesn't talk about pets going to heaven, but it does talk about being happy there. Seeing your pet in heaven would make you happy. C. S. Lewis, a university professor and the author of The Chronicles of Narnia series, believed pets go to heaven. He might have based this belief on the description in Isaiah 11:6: "The wolf will live with the lamb, the leopard will lie down with the goat, the calf and the lion and the yearling together; and a little child will lead them."

Are angels real?

Angels are mentioned in the Bible many times. They are messengers from God who tell us important things and keep us safe from harm. Angels appear in dreams or when people are awake. They are often described as wearing long white robes. Some fly in the air with feathered wings. Some might be disguised as people on Earth, like Hebrews 13:2 describes: "Do not forget to show hospitality to strangers, for by so doing some people have shown hospitality to angels without knowing it." In one Bible story, Daniel was trapped in a den with hungry lions. An angel protected Daniel, and the lions didn't hurt him. Psalm 91:11 says, "For he will command his angels concerning you to guard you in all your ways."

What is hell?

Some Christians believe hell is a place beneath the earth where Satan lives to punish evil people after they die. It sounds scary! But other Christians cannot believe that a loving God would send anyone to such a place. They believe hell is a state of being separated or apart from God after we die. Isaiah 59:2 talks about what keeps us apart from God: "But your iniquities have separated you from your God; your sins have hidden his face from you, so that he will not hear." Iniquities are sins or wickedness. Jesus saves us from sin, so we will not be separated from God.

Who is Satan?

Some people think of Satan, also called "the devil," as a person dressed in red or black with horns. Many people believe Satan is not a person but a symbol for evil. Evil is the opposite of good. In the Bible, Satan was a cherub, or angel, but wanted to become God to rule Earth, so he turned against God. 1 John 3:8 says, "The one who does what is sinful is of the devil, because the devil has been sinning from the beginning. The reason the Son of God appeared was to destroy the devil's work." Jesus saves us from Satan in the way that He saves us from evil.

 **If there were a fight between God and Satan, who would win?**

 God is good. He tells the truth and doesn't trick you or tempt you to do something wrong. God cares about people and animals. Satan is a symbol for evil. Evil is bad. Satan lies, tricks, and tempts you to sin. He doesn't care about people or animals. Satan is strong, but God is stronger. In a fight between God and Satan, almighty God would win. Good always wins over evil. Revelation 19:6 says, "Then I heard what sounded like a great multitude, like the roar of rushing waters and like loud peals of thunder, shouting: 'Hallelujah! For our Lord God Almighty reigns.'"

Why do we pray?

We don't just pray to ask for something or to tell God something we have done wrong. We pray to thank God. We pray to praise God. Most important, we pray to have a friendship or relationship with God. Prayer is a way we talk to God, like we would to a trusted friend. God wants us to pray instead of worry. Philippians 4:6 tells us, "Do not be anxious about anything, but in every situation, by prayer and petition, with thanksgiving, present your requests to God." You can pray about everything in your life. Praying can give you a peaceful feeling like no other!

How can God hear everyone's prayers?

Have you tried to hear what someone is saying when everyone is talking at once? It's too noisy! It's hard to imagine God hearing everyone praying at the same time. But God isn't one person in a crowded room. We live in one body, but God doesn't. Think of air. It's everywhere, but we don't see it. God is everywhere, but we don't see Him. God isn't human like we are. He can hear everything. Job 34:21 explains, "His eyes are on the ways of mortals; he sees their every step."

Will God answer my prayers?

God will answer your prayers, but the answer might take longer than you want. It's important to be persistent. That means keep trying. Matthew 7:7 says, "Ask and it will be given to you; seek and you will find; knock and the door will be opened to you." The door is a symbol. It will be opened if you keep knocking. Keep asking, seeking, and knocking. In other words, keep praying. Bible stories show prayers are answered when people persist. The Bible says that Hannah, for example, prayed for many years, asking, seeking, and knocking, and her prayer finally came true. The answer might not be what you expect, but your prayer will be answered!

Do prayers work?

Many stories in the Bible show that prayers work. Hezekiah, king of Judah, for example, was very sick. He prayed to God and was healed. But sometimes when you pray, nothing happens. It seems like your prayer isn't working. But that's when God is working behind the scenes. Romans 8:28 says, "And we know that in all things God works for the good of those who love him, who have been called according to his purpose." That doesn't mean your prayer always works the way you want it to. It might work in a surprising way, or it might be better than you could have imagined!

Why aren't prayers for my sick friend working?

God knows you are praying for your friend. Psalm 66:19 says, "But God has surely listened and has heard my prayer." God heard your prayer. That's comforting. It's sad to see anyone you love sick. You want your prayers to work so your friend will be well. It's hard to understand why some people get well and others don't. Have you thought of following up prayers with actions? Pray your friend is comfortable, and offer to bring snacks or flowers. Pray they have company, and sit with them. Pray they know that they are loved, and tell them so. Those prayers are working.

Is there a best way to pray?

When you pray, you open your heart to God. Praying helps you know that you are not alone. It helps you know God's love. You can thank God in a prayer. You can tell God, or confess, something you did wrong. You can ask for something for yourself or someone else. Jesus taught a prayer in Matthew 6:9–13. It's called the Lord's Prayer. In it, Jesus calls God His "Father": "Our Father in heaven, hallowed be your name, your kingdom come, your will be done, on earth as it is in heaven" (Matthew 6:9–10). "Hallowed" means holy. You can recite a specific prayer like that or make up your own. It can be out loud or silent. Any way you pray is the best way!

What is the best time and place to pray?

Some people pray in the morning. Some people pray at night before they go to bed. Some say grace, a prayer before they eat. People say prayers at church. Some are said aloud, while others are said silently. Just before Jesus taught the Lord's Prayer, He told His followers not to pray for the sake of getting attention from other people. Some prayers should be said in private. In Matthew 6:6, Jesus calls God "Father" and says, "But when you pray, go into your room, close the door and pray to your Father, who is unseen. Then your Father, who sees what is done in secret, will reward you." Whenever and wherever you want to pray is the best time and place!

Do I have to kneel to pray?

God will accept any way you pray, even if you can't kneel. If you can, kneeling can help you focus on the way you think or feel about something. Your attitude leads to your behavior. The right attitude for prayer is respect and honor. Kneeling can prepare your heart and mind. You respect God when you kneel, bow your head, or raise your arms. In Jeremiah 29:12–13, God talks about prayer: "Then you will call on me and come and pray to me, and I will listen to you. You will seek me and find me when you seek me with all your heart."

Can God hear a prayer I say silently?

Psalm 139:4 says, "Before a word is on my tongue you, Lord, know it completely." God not only knows your thoughts, but He also understands them. You don't have to say a prayer out loud for God to hear it. You can pray silently anytime, anywhere, and God will be by your side. Sometimes prayers are so precious that you don't want to say them out loud. God can still hear and answer you. It's a comfort to know that He knows what is in your heart.

Why should I pray if God already knows my prayer?

God wants you to talk to Him! He wants to have a relationship with you. He wants you to share your thoughts and prayers, like you would with someone close to you. Don't you like it when a friend relies on you or asks for your help? God wants you to trust and rely on Him. When you tell God your prayers, it helps God, and it helps you, too. Jesus encourages us in Mark 11:24: "Therefore I tell you, whatever you ask for in prayer, believe that you have received it, and it will be yours."

Is it wrong to pray for toys?

God wants you to be happy. He wants you to have toys to play with. But God wants you to have the right attitude, too. God doesn't want you to be greedy. Being greedy means wanting a lot more of something, like food or money, much more than you need. God wants you to care more about people than things. That might mean praying for the strength to carry on without something you want. 1 Thessalonians 5:16–17 says, "Rejoice always, pray continually." God wants you to be happy and pray all the time. There is no prayer too small. If there is a toy you want, you can ask for it in prayer.

Is it wrong to pray for good grades in school?

It's okay to pray for good grades. But you need to follow through with action. Praying for good grades can help you listen in class, do the reading, and study for tests. You can't wait for God to give you the answers, though. Praying will help show you what is needed in order for your prayer to come true. Romans 12:12 says, "Be joyful in hope, patient in affliction, faithful in prayer." You can find joy in the work. You can be patient when it takes time. That doesn't mean it won't be hard. Praying will help guide you to succeed.

Did Jesus pray?

Yes, Jesus prayed. Mark 1:35 tells us, "Very early in the morning, while it was still dark, Jesus got up, left the house and went off to a solitary place, where he prayed." A solitary place is one where you are alone. Jesus had been with crowds of people. He had healed many sick people. Jesus needed to get away. He wanted to be alone with God to pray. Jesus took time away from His work and His friends. Jesus showed how important it is to make the time to pray and to find a place to talk to God.

What is the Bible?

The Bible is a collection of holy books, inspired by God, that have been bound into one big book. This sacred text has two main parts, the Old Testament and the New Testament. Some Christians believe every word of the Bible is true. Some Christians believe the Bible is true but contains some stories and examples and is not 100 percent word-for-word truth. Hebrews 4:12 calls the Bible "the word of God": "For the word of God is alive and active. Sharper than any double-edged sword, it penetrates even to dividing soul and spirit, joints and marrow; it judges the thoughts and attitudes of the heart."

What is the Old Testament?

The Old Testament is a collection of books in the Bible, written over a thousand years before Christ was born. The first book, Genesis, talks about the creation of the world. One book, Proverbs, is a collection of wise sayings. Other books contain laws, history, and wisdom. Some of them were written by prophets who shared God's message. The Old Testament, sometimes called the Hebrew Bible, is the sacred text of the Jewish religion. Jesus read and studied the Hebrew Bible. Psalm 119:105 talks about the Word of God being a lamp, meaning the words help guide you: "Your word is a lamp for my feet, a light on my path."

What is the New Testament?

The New Testament was put together after Jesus died. The first four books in the New Testament focus on Jesus's life and His teachings. They are called the Gospels. The book of Acts tells how the apostles spread Jesus's message after He ascended. Some books are letters, or Epistles, to church leaders and followers. The last book, Revelation, includes visions of a world saved by God's goodness. John 3:16 is a summary of the New Testament: "For God so loved the world that he gave his one and only Son, that whoever believes in him shall not perish but have eternal life."

What are "psalms"?

Psalms are songs and prayers. Psalms is also a book in the Old Testament containing 150 of them. Many psalms praise God, thanking Him and showing Him respect. Other psalms call out to God in anger, sadness, or fear. It's helpful to read them aloud. They express how the person writing the psalm felt. David, one of Jesus's ancestors, wrote many of the psalms. The last psalm says to celebrate God with dancing and musical instruments, like a harp and flute. Psalm 150:6 says, "Let everything that has breath praise the Lord. Praise the Lord."

What are the Ten Commandments?

The Ten Commandments are a list of ten rules that God gave to Moses. They include what you should do, such as worshipping only (one) God and honoring your parents. They also say what you should not do, like kill, steal, and lie. God wants you to know and live by these important rules. Deuteronomy 6:6 says, "These commandments that I give you today are to be on your hearts." To be "on your heart" means that you know and keep these commandments in mind.

What did Jesus say was the most important commandment?

In Matthew 22:37, "Jesus replied: 'Love the Lord your God with all your heart and with all your soul and with all your mind.'" Loving God is the first and most important commandment. Jesus added that the second-greatest commandment is to love your neighbor as yourself. It's hard to love anyone else if you don't love yourself. Your neighbor is not only the person who lives next door but also every person you know. Jesus said if we believe in and live by these two commandments, we will keep all the other commandments.

What is the Golden Rule, and why should I follow it?

Something that is "golden" is good, or pleasing, or favorable. The Golden Rule says to treat other people the way you want them to treat you. So, let's say you were playing a game in class, and a kid you didn't know asked if they could play. You might not want them to, but you let them play with you. That's how you would want to be treated; you would want someone to let you play. Matthew 7:12 states the Golden Rule: "So in everything, do to others what you would have them do to you, for this sums up the Law and the Prophets."

Why should I read the Bible?

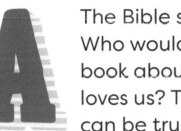

The Bible shows us God's love. Who wouldn't want to read a book about how much someone loves us? The stories show God can be trusted. Reading the Bible helps increase your faith in God. The Bible contains wisdom, guidance, and salvation. It brings joy, peace, and understanding. Romans 15:4 talks about the importance of reading the Bible: "For everything that was written in the past was written to teach us, so that through the endurance taught in the Scriptures and the encouragement they provide we might have hope."

What is Scripture?

The words of the Bible are also called "Scripture." Scripture is sacred, or holy, writing inspired by God. The Bible is divided into books. Each book is divided into chapters, which are then divided into verses. The first number after a Bible book is the chapter. The second number (after the colon) is the verse. This makes verses easy to find. A Bible verse is also called "Scripture." For example, "2 Timothy 3:16–17" is read as "the second book of Timothy, chapter 3, verses 16 through 17." These verses say, "All Scripture is God-breathed and is useful for teaching, rebuking, correcting and training in righteousness, so that the servant of God may be thoroughly equipped for every good work."

Why should I memorize Bible verses?

Just like you can sing a song that you've memorized whenever you want, if you know a Bible verse by heart, you can think of it at any time. Bible verses give you strength when you need it. They guide you to do what is right. They give comfort when you are sad. Memorizing Bible verses Is easy for some people but hard for others. You might memorize Bible verses for a church class, or you might want to try to remember them on your own. Psalm 119:11 reveals the great benefit of memorization: "I have hidden your word in my heart that I might not sin against you."

What does the Bible say about looking to God for strength to do the right thing?

Philippians 4:13 says, "I can do all this through him who gives me strength." God gives strength for your body and your mind. God gives strength for big things and for small everyday things. It's not easy to wake up early. Rely on God. It's not easy to stop playing to clean your room. Ask God for help. It's not easy to be nice when someone isn't nice to you. God can help you be nice even when you don't feel like you can be. God can help you do anything. Believe in God, and use His strength as your own.

 **How can the Bible help me through tough times?**

 Are you afraid of the dark, being alone, or big storms? Everyone is afraid sometimes. Over and over again the Bible says, "Do not be afraid." Why? Because God is here. God is with you. Believe the words in Isaiah 41:10: "So do not fear, for I am with you; do not be dismayed, for I am your God. I will strengthen you and help you; I will uphold you with my righteous right hand." God says not to be "dismayed," or upset. He will keep you safe.

God's "righteous right hand" is good and all-powerful! Try looking for strength in the Bible. Some Bibles offer lists of Scripture verses to help you in any situation.

Why do we go to church?

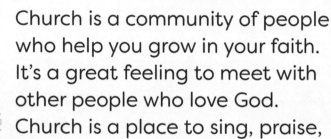

Church is a community of people who help you grow in your faith. It's a great feeling to meet with other people who love God. Church is a place to sing, praise, and worship God. Church is a place to pray, hear Bible stories, and make friends. Church is a place to learn about God and Jesus. Hebrews 10:24–25 says that when we meet together, good things happen: "And let us consider how we may spur one another on toward love and good deeds, not giving up meeting together, as some are in the habit of doing, but encouraging one another."

What is a church family?

Your church family is anyone who works at or attends your church. Your church family includes everyone, from the oldest person to a newborn baby. It includes *you*! People in your church family belong to the same religion. They have beliefs like yours. Having a church family is like having extra grandmas, grandpas, aunts, uncles, and cousins. It's like having a big, loving, extended family outside of your caregivers and siblings (and pets!). Psalm 133:1 says, "How good and pleasant it is when God's people live together in unity!"

How can I praise God?

Praising God is thanking Him for what He has done. It's expressing a joyful, deep-down happiness. So, when you praise, feel free to move! Cheer and clap your hands to thank God for all He has given you. Sing and count your many blessings. Praise God for hearing your prayers. Praise God for His love. Do a dance. Beat a drum. Ring a bell. Or simply say a silent prayer of gratitude. James 5:13 says, "Is anyone among you in trouble? Let them pray. Is anyone happy? Let them sing songs of praise." Praising God feels good!

How can I worship God?

Praising God is one way to worship. But worshipping God goes deeper than celebrating God for all He has done. Worshipping God is thanking Him for who He is. God is amazing! In worship, you show honor and respect for God. You might bow your head to say a prayer or raise your arms to sing. Or you might show Him respect by doing good things, not just using your words. Try to forget about yourself and focus on God. In 2 Samuel 7:22, David says, "How great you are, Sovereign Lord! There is no one like you, and there is no God but you, as we have heard with our own ears." Saying that Scripture out loud is one easy way to worship.

Can church be outside?

Jesus preached outside to thousands of people. In Matthew 18:20, Jesus said, "For where two or three gather in my name, there am I with them." That means it doesn't matter where you are; Jesus can be there with you. A church building has everything people need to worship, like places to sit, a microphone, and heat or air-conditioning. But it's fun to be outside! Some Easter church services are held by a lake or in a park early in the morning. You can watch the sun rise. Inside or outside, what's important is coming together to worship God.

Why do we take Holy Communion?

Jesus was eating supper for the last time with His friends, the disciples. He was eating in communion with them, meaning He was sharing with them. Jesus knew He was going to die and wanted it to be a special meal. Mark 14:22 says, "While they were eating, Jesus took bread, and when he had given thanks, he broke it and gave it to his disciples." Today, Holy Communion is bread or a wafer that reminds us of the sacrifice Jesus made in giving His life for us.

What does Jesus say about tithing?

Tithing is giving or donating a percentage of what you have to the church, a tenth to be exact. Let's say you have ten apples. To tithe, you'd keep nine and give one to the church. Long ago, grains or fruits were given to the Lord. Today, people give money to the church instead of goods. In Luke 11:42 Jesus scolded the religious leaders: "Woe to you Pharisees, because you give God a tenth of your mint, rue and all other kinds of garden herbs, but you neglect justice and the love of God. You should have practiced the latter without leaving the former undone." The leaders tithed, but they forgot justice. Jesus reminded them about what's important: treating people fairly.

What holidays do Christians celebrate?

The word "holiday" comes from two words, "holy" and "day." On these days we take time to think about a holiday's true meaning and celebrate with others who have the same beliefs. Christians celebrate a number of holidays, but the most important are Christmas and Easter. Christmas celebrates Jesus's birth. Easter celebrates Jesus's resurrection, when He rose from the dead. Each holiday has its own traditions. Both have a holy period of time before them to allow us to get ready for these holidays. Advent is a time to prepare for Christmas. Lent is a time to prepare for Easter. Psalm 145:7 says of celebrating God, "They celebrate your abundant goodness and joyfully sing of your righteousness."

What is Advent?

"Advent" means "coming." What's coming? Christmas! Advent is an exciting time of anticipation. It begins about four weeks before December 25. People get ready in different ways. Children open windows on Advent calendars or decorate Advent trees (called Jesse trees) to count down the days. Special candles in Advent wreaths are lit. Special prayers are said. Some people bake cookies or special breads and cakes. In Luke 3:4, people prepared for Jesus, too: "As it is written in the book of the words of Isaiah the prophet: 'A voice of one calling in the wilderness, "Prepare the way for the Lord, make straight paths for him."'"

What does Christmas celebrate?

Think of how excited you feel near your birthday. You expect good things to happen. That's how people feel about Christmas. It's Jesus's birthday! The nativity story tells the good news of Jesus's birth, when God came to live on Earth. Christmas brings great hope of being closer to God through His Son, Jesus. Luke 2:11 tells us it's the day Jesus was born, "Today in the town of David a Savior has been born to you; he is the Messiah, the Lord."

Is Christmas the day Jesus was born?

We celebrate the birth of Jesus on December 25, but that's not the actual date Jesus was born. The Bible doesn't list the day, month, or year. Some people think it was in January; others think it was in September. Long ago, they didn't celebrate birthdays the way we do now. It wasn't until about three hundred years after Jesus died that people started celebrating His birthday on December 25. The date doesn't really matter; what's more important is celebrating the birth of the Son of God! In Luke 2:10, an angel talking about Jesus's birth says, "I bring you good news that will cause great joy for all the people."

Why was Jesus born in a stable?

Jesus's parents, Mary and Joseph, traveled to Bethlehem. The inns were full, so Mary and Joseph slept with animals in a stable to keep warm. When Jesus was born, He was placed in a manger (a wood or stone box that holds food for animals) because they didn't have a crib. Christians believe this was a symbol: Jesus is food for our spirits. Luke 2:7 says, "And she gave birth to her firstborn, a son. She wrapped him in cloths and placed him in a manger, because there was no guest room available for them."

Why do we give gifts on Christmas?

People celebrate birthdays by giving gifts. Giving gifts shows we care. We celebrate Jesus's birthday that way, too, in memory of when important men called the Magi, or the Wise Men, gave baby Jesus birthday gifts. While it's fun to receive gifts, it's also fun to give gifts. The Bible says it's better to give gifts than to receive them. Acts 20:35 says, "In everything I did, I showed you that by this kind of hard work we must help the weak, remembering the words the Lord Jesus himself said: 'It is more blessed to give than to receive.'"

 **Is Santa Claus a Christian?**

 The idea of Santa Claus comes from Saint Nicholas. Nicholas was born long ago in Greece, around AD 280. He was a bishop, an important person in the Christian Catholic church, who became a saint after he died. A saint is a holy person. The legend of Saint Nicholas tells how he enjoyed giving gifts to children. 2 Corinthians 9:7 says, "Each of you should give what you have decided in your heart to give, not reluctantly or under compulsion, for God loves a cheerful giver."

What is Lent?

Lent begins forty days (not counting Sundays) before Easter. Why forty days? Jesus spent forty days in the desert fasting and praying. Lent is a time to reflect on, or think carefully about, your life. Lent is a time to ask for forgiveness. People often give up something during Lent, which is making a sacrifice. Lent is a time to think about Jesus's sacrifice for us—Jesus gave up His life, after all. Ephesians 5:2 says, "And walk in the way of love, just as Christ loved us and gave himself up for us as a fragrant offering and sacrifice to God."

What is fasting?

When someone fasts, they don't eat. But our bodies need food to live. So people either don't eat certain foods or don't eat at certain times. Doctors say it's not healthy for children to fast until they are eighteen years old or older. People often fast during Lent and use that time to pray. Some people think fasting helps them feel closer to God. People deny their bodies food so they can feed their spirits through prayer and worship. Luke 2:37 describes a prophet named Anna: "She never left the temple but worshiped night and day, fasting and praying." When Anna met baby Jesus, she immediately knew He was the Messiah.

Why is the Sunday before Easter called Palm Sunday?

People waved and placed palm branches in front of Jesus as He rode into Jerusalem on a donkey. They did this the week before He died. His followers placed the palms in His path as a symbol of victory. John 12:13 tells us, "They took palm branches and went out to meet him, shouting 'Hosanna!' 'Blessed is he who comes in the name of the Lord!' 'Blessed is the king of Israel!'" They knew Jesus was going to save them! Today, many churches use real palms in their services the week before Easter to reenact the event. The palms are blessed by a priest, saved, and used in church services the following year.

What is Easter?

Easter is a joyous celebration! People dress up, go to church, and have parades. Why? Jesus is alive! On Easter, we celebrate Jesus being resurrected, or brought back to life. Three days before that, Jesus was crucified, meaning He was nailed to a wooden cross, and He died. (That's how the Romans punished people long ago. It's against the law now.) Easter fulfills God's promise. Jesus died for our sins so we would be forgiven. Romans 6:23 says, "For the wages of sin is death, but the gift of God is eternal life in Christ Jesus our Lord."

Write Your Own Questions

You've read lots of questions, but I'm sure you have some of your own. Use this space to write them down. Read them with a trusted adult. You can find the answers together!

....

....

....

....

....

....

....

....

....

....

....

Discussion Guide for Parents

This book is intended to be a jumping-off point for discussions. There's space in the previous section for children to write their own questions about Christianity and God. Here are some ways to help continue those conversations and to seek answers together.

Family Discussions

The dinner table is a great place to have discussions because you can hear answers from several different people. At the end of dinner, ask your child to read one of their journal questions out loud. Give everyone a chance to answer. Then have your child come up with their own answer, reflecting on what everyone else said.

Sit on the sofa with your child to research an answer to one of their questions. Look on your computer or phone. For example, if you want to see what the Bible says about happiness, type "Bible verses on happiness" in the search bar. Click on different sites and read through the answers. Discuss the answers. What does your child think? Your child can write down an answer they like.

Another great time for a one-on-one conversation is while you're traveling with your child to and from school and other activities. You can ask your child to bring this book along and read a question. You can discuss the question and possible answers. Then ask your child about the answer they think is best.

A good time to talk together is after your child is ready for bed. Ask your child to read a question. You can ask what they think and then give your thoughts. During this quiet time, you might pray with your child for help finding the answer to their question. Or, you might lead a prayer of thanks for the answer(s) you found. Seeing you pray proudly is a great way to encourage your child and keep them praying!

Resources

Bible Gateway is a website for adults with a searchable database of Bible translations: biblegateway.com.

CEB Deep Blue Kids Bible is a Bible with interactive features for seven- to twelve-year-olds.

For Everyone Bible Study Guides by N. T. Wright is a series of commentary books for adults.

Got Questions is a website for adults that provides biblical answers to spiritual questions: gotquestions.org.

I Wonder: Engaging a Child's Curiosity about the Bible by Elizabeth Caldwell is a book for adults about engaging children's curiosity about the Bible.

Making Sense of the Bible: Rediscovering the Power of Scripture Today by Adam Hamilton is a book for adults on understanding difficult issues.

NIV Action Study Bible, illustrated by Sergio Cariello, is a Bible with comic book–style illustrations for eight- to twelve-year-olds.

NIV Kids' Visual Study Bible is a Bible with many illustrations for eight- to twelve-year-olds.

The NIV Study Bible by Kenneth L. Barker is a Bible for adults with commentary.

References

Abbott, Shari. "Was Jesus Born in a Stable, a Cave or a House?" Reasons for Hope Jesus. December 8, 2014. reasonsforhopejesus.com/was-jesus-born-in-a-stable-cave-house.

Austin, Michael W. "Why Beliefs Matter: On the Processes and Significance of Belief." *Psychology Today*. January 24, 2011. psychologytoday.com/us/blog/ethics-everyone/201101/why-beliefs-matter.

BBC. "The Death of Jesus." Accessed January 25, 2022. bbc.co.uk/bitesize/guides/z6b96v4/revision/8.

BBC. "Lent." Last updated June 22, 2009. bbc.co.uk/religion/religions/christianity/holydays/lent_1.shtml.

Britannica Encyclopaedia. "Bible." Last updated March 11, 2022. britannica.com/topic/Bible.

Britannica Encyclopaedia. "Satan." Accessed January 3, 2022. britannica.com/topic/Satan.

Ellis, Sam. "Apostle vs Disciple: What's the Difference?" Catholics & Bible. August 23, 2021. catholicsbible.com/apostle-vs-disciple.

Handwerk, Brian. "From St. Nicholas to Santa Claus: The Surprising Origins of Kris Kringle." *National Geographic*. December 25, 2018. nationalgeographic.com/history/article/131219-santa-claus-origin-history-christmas-facts-st-nicholas.

Hillerbrand, Hans J. "Christmas." *Encyclopaedia Britannica*. Last updated October 25, 2021. britannica.com/topic/Christmas.

Johns Hopkins Medicine. "Intermittent Fasting: What Is It, and How Does It Work?" Accessed March 1, 2022. hopkinsmedicine.org/health/wellness-and-prevention/intermittent-fasting-what-is-it-and-how-does-it-work.

Mayo Clinic. "Positive Thinking: Stop Negative Self-Talk to Reduce Stress." February 3, 2022. mayoclinic.org/healthy-lifestyle/stress -management/in-depth/positive-thinking/art-20043950.

Murphy, Caryle. "Most Americans Believe in Heaven . . . and Hell." November 10, 2015. pewresearch.org/fact-tank/2015/11/10 /most-americans-believe-in-heaven-and-hell.

Roos, Dave. "When Was Jesus Really Born? Not Dec. 25." December 23, 2021. people.howstuffworks.com/when-was -jesus-born.htm.

Seet, Charles. "Luke 19:41–44—Why Did Christ Weep over the City?" Life Bible-Presbyterian Church. March 20, 2005. lifebpc .com/index.php/resources/treasury-of-sermons/65-luke/419 -luke-19-41-44-why-did-christ-weep-over-the-city.

Shlemon, Alan. "How Is Christianity Different from Other Religions?" September 18, 2017. Stand to Reason. str.org/w/how-is -christianity-different-from-other-religions-.

Strauss, Valerie. "Why Is Christmas on Dec. 25? (It Wasn't Always.)" *Washington Post*. December 24, 2014. washingtonpost.com /news/answer-sheet/wp/2014/12/24/why-is-christmas-on -dec-25-it-wasnt-always.

Index

Salvation (*continued*)
    being saved, describing, 53
    grace of salvation, 60
    Jesus as spreading the
        word on, 42
Santa Claus, 105
Satan (the devil), 64, 65, 66
School, 78
Scripture. *See under* Bible
Service to others, 36, 37
Sin, 15, 21, 64
    describing and
        defining, 58
    forgiveness from sin, 17,
        40, 53, 54
    heart of God, our sins as
        troubling, 14
    Jesus as dying for our sins,
        40, 51, 109

Satan as associated
    with, 65, 66
transgressions as, 16
verses of the Bible as a
    shield against, 89

T
Ten Commandments, 84
Tithing, 98
Trinity, 28

W
Worship, 48, 96, 107
    church, worship done
        in, 49, 92
    of God, 3, 49, 50, 84
    ways to worship, 95

About the Author

 **Amy Houts** is an award-winning author of over one hundred books for children, including *God's Protection Covers Me* (Beaming Books), *The Giant Book of Bible Fingerplays for Preschoolers* (Group Publishing), and *Active Bible Play* (David C Cook). Amy and her husband Steve are members of the United Methodist Church, where Amy has attended Bible study for thirty years. They live in rural northwest Missouri near Steve's family's farm. They share God's love with their two grown daughters and three grandchildren.

Printed in the USA
CPSIA information can be obtained
at www.ICGtesting.com
LVHW072329160923
758025LV00005B/37